BOOM SCIENCE

PLANTS

Georgia Amson-Bradshaw

WAYLAND
www.waylandbooks.co.uk

Published in paperback in Great Britain in 2019 by Wayland

Copyright © Hodder and Stoughton Limited, 2018

Produced for Wayland by
White-Thomson Publishing Ltd
www.wtpub.co.uk

Series Editor: Georgia Amson-Bradshaw
Series Designer: Rocket Design (East Anglia) Ltd

ISBN: 978 1 5263 0633 3
10 9 8 7 6 5 4 3 2 1

Wayland
An imprint of
Hachette Children's Group
Part of Hodder & Stoughton
Carmelite House
50 Victoria Embankment
London EC4Y 0DZ

An Hachette UK Company
www.hachette.co.uk
www.hachettechildrens.co.uk

Printed in China

Picture acknowledgements:
Images from Shutterstock.com: Tatjana Romanova 7l, Vaclav Volrab 7r, ANURAKE SINGTO-ON 7br, Nikitina Olga 8, moryachok 9tl, Food_asia 9c, shubin42 9, Anastasiia 9, Skorobogatova 13t, Christine C Brooks 13l, Gracy Oliver 13b udaix 14, kc_film 15c, Ian Fletcher 15b, ensiferum 16l, nafanya241 16b, Maria_OH 17t, Anastasiia Skorobogatova 17b, Sergey Chirkov 18b, Richard Griffin 19, Zerbor 23l, Sanit Fuangnakhon 23, rsooll 23b, luckypic 24t, DK Arts 24b, Esin Deniz 25b.
All illustrations on pages 10, 11, 20, 21, 26, 27 by Steve Evans

All design elements from Shutterstock.

Glossary words are shown in bold.

CONTENTS

PLANTS

Plants are living things that come in many shapes and sizes.

Who wants a hug from a cactus?

BIG, SMALL, HARD, SOFT

There are many different kinds of plant, from tiny cress to giant trees. Cactus plants are hard and spiky. Grass plants are soft and brushy.

WOW!

The tallest tree in the world is a redwood tree. It is 115 metres tall. That's as tall as a skyscraper!

FLOWER POWER

Most plants have **flowers**. These are called **flowering plants**. Some plants do not have flowers. These are called **non-flowering plants**.

A fern is a non-flowering plant.

A crocus is a flowering plant.

HIDE AND SEEK

A daisy is a small, white flowering plant. How many can you spot hiding?

HEY, WHAT AM I?

What sort of plant is this? Answer on page 28.

ROOTS AND STEMS

Roots anchor a plant in the ground, and a stem holds it up.

STRONG STEMS

The **stem** is the part of the plant that supports the **leaves** and flowers. Some stems are very big. A tree's **trunk** is its main stem.

←- - - - stem

roots

HIDING UNDERGROUND

The **roots** are the part of the plant you don't normally see, because they are buried in the soil. They hold the plant firmly in the ground.

SLURP!

THIRSTY LEAVES

Stems have hollow tubes, like straws, inside them. The tubes carry water and **nutrients** from the roots to the leaves and the flowers.

WOW!

Tree roots are very strong. They can even crack tarmac as they grow!

HAIRY ROOTS

Roots are covered in tiny hairs. The hairs suck up water and nutrients from the soil.

HEY, WHAT AM I?

What can you see in this picture? Answer on page 28.

COLOUR CHANGE CELERY

Prove that stems carry water up to the leaves. You'll need:

A bunch of celery with leaves

Three glasses of water

Three colours of food dye

STEP ONE

Put a few drops of food dye into each glass of water and mix. Blue, red and yellow food dyes work well.

STEP €O

Separate three sticks of celery from the bunch, and trim them across the bottom.

STEP THREE

Place a stick of celery in each glass and leave them for 24 hours.

How do the leaves look after a day?

STEP FOUR

Ask an adult to cut widthways across the stems to reveal the insides of the stems. What can you see?

LEAVES

Leaves are where plants turn sunlight into food.

Howzat!

SUN CATCHER

The job of a leaf is to catch sunlight. Sunlight contains energy that plants turn into sugars that they use as food. Leaves are spread out along a plant's stem to catch as much light as possible.

HIDE AND SEEK

A holly leaf is dark green and spiky. Can you find TWO holly leaves hiding?

HEY, WHAT AM I?

Which plant's leaves are these?
Answer on page 28.

SEEING GREEN

Most leaves are green, but they come in lots of different shapes and sizes.

Cheese plant leaves have holes in, like Swiss cheese!

Clover leaves are heart-shaped.

EAT YOUR GREENS

Leaves are an important food for many animals, including humans. We eat lettuce leaves and spinach leaves in salads. We use the leaves of herb plants like parsley and basil for flavouring.

FLOWERS

The flower is where seeds are made.

PARTS OF A FLOWER

Most plants have flowers. Each part of a flower has a job.

Petals are colourful. It is the job of the petals to attract insects.

The job of the **anthers** is to hold **pollen**.

The **style** is topped with a sticky pad called the **stigma**. The stigma receives pollen from other flowers.

The **ovary** is where new **seeds** grow.

POLLEN SWAP

A plant needs to receive pollen from another flower of the same **species** in order to create new seeds. Visiting insects carry pollen between flowers.

BUZZ
BUZZ

Insects can see colours that humans can't. Some flowers have 'bullseyes' for insects in colours that are invisible to us!

Bees see this.

We see this.

HEY, WHAT AM I?

What are the orange parts of this flower called? Answer on page 28.

FRUIT

Fruit protect and carry the seeds.

FLOWER TO FRUIT

Once a flower has received pollen from another flower, the petals fall off. The ovary, where the new seeds are growing, gets bigger and turns into a fruit.

Flowers turn into fruit.

SEED CARRIER

A fruit has two jobs. The first job is to protect the seeds as they are growing. The second is to move the seeds away from the plant when they are grown.

(!) SEEDS INSIDE (!)
HANDLE WITH CARE

JUICY FRUIT

Fruit move seeds away from the plant with the help of animals. Birds and animals eat tasty fruit with seeds inside. The seeds pass through the animals and are left behind in their droppings.

Yum!

WOW!

Pomegranate fruits can contain over 1,000 seeds!

SEED SUCCESS

In the wild, lots of seeds end up somewhere they can't grow. Some fruit contain lots of seeds to make sure at least some will be successful.

SEEDS AND BULBS

New plants grow from seeds or bulbs.

SUPER SEEDLINGS

Seeds need water, **oxygen** and warmth to sprout into a new plant. They shoot little roots downwards, and a stem upwards. This is called a **seedling**.

A seed is planted.

The seed starts to sprout.

The root and stem start to form.

A seedling is a mini plant.

GONE WITH THE WIND

Another way that plants spread their seeds is using the wind. A dandelion seed has little feathery 'wings' that catch the wind and carry the seed far away.

dandelion seeds

BRIGHT BULBS

Some plants, such as daffodils, grow from **bulbs**. Bulbs are like little brown paper packages containing all the food needed to grow a plant.

New bulbs, called **bulblets**, grow on the side of the original bulb, then split off.

HEY, WHAT AM I?

What can you see in this picture? Answer on page 29.

HIDE AND SEEK

Can you spot a dandelion seed that has blown somewhere on this page?

GROW A BULB IN WATER

See how a bulb sprouts into a brand new plant. You'll need:

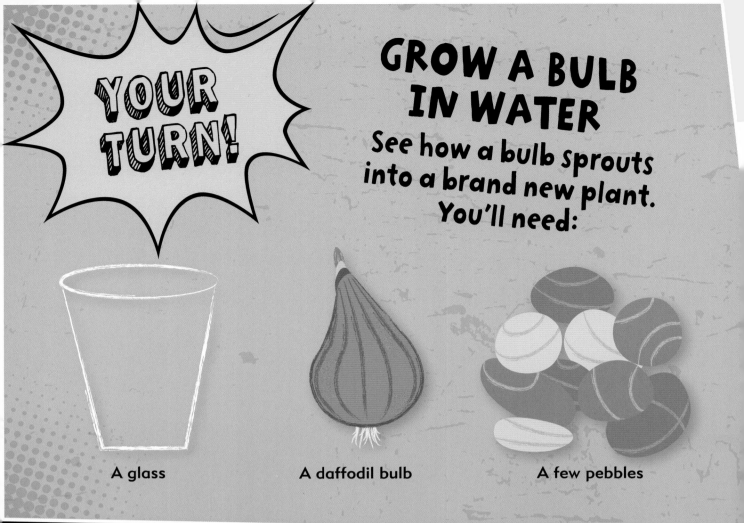

A glass

A daffodil bulb

A few pebbles

STEP ONE

Put the pebbles in the bottom of the glass and sit the daffodil bulb on top, pointy side up. Add water to the glass until the water is just below the bottom of the bulb, but the bulb is left dry.

STEP €0

What grows first? Roots or shoots?

Leave your bulb in a bright spot, but out of direct sunlight, for a few weeks, and watch it grow. Make sure you regularly top up the water to the same level.

TAKE IT FURTHER

If you are very good at waiting and have a garden, you could plant out your bulb. Check with your grown-up first though!

After your daffodil has finished blooming, trim off the leaves and flower from the bulb. Dig a hole in the soil about 15 cm deep, and sprinkle some **fertiliser** inside. Pop the bulb in the hole and cover it up.

In one or two years the daffodil should bloom again. The plant will grow new bulblets under the soil.

SUNLIGHT
All plants need sunlight to grow.

HUNGRY FOR SUN

Plants use sunlight, water and **carbon dioxide** from the air to make food for themselves. This is called **photosynthesis**.

$$\text{sun} + \text{water} + CO_2 = \text{tree}$$

SHADY BUSINESS

Trees try to spread their seeds far and wide. This is because new seedlings need sunlight. They can't grow well in the shade of the **mature** tree.

You're blocking my light!

LOSING LEAVES

Because there is less sunlight in winter, some trees drop their leaves. These are called **deciduous trees**. Trees that don't drop all their leaves in winter are called **evergreen trees**.

An oak is a deciduous tree.

A pine is an evergreen tree.

HIDE AND SEEK

Some trees' leaves go yellow or red before they drop. Can you spot a red maple leaf?

HEY, WHAT AM I?

What can you see in this picture? Answer on page 29.

WATER AND WARMTH

Like us, plants need water and warmth to stay healthy.

NEED A DRINK?

All plants need water, but some plants need more than others. Plants such as banana trees that grow in rainy, tropical areas need lots of water.

WOW!

Cactus plants can live for several years without water! During rare desert rainstorms, they suck up as much water as possible. They live off the stored water until the next rainstorm.

SLEEPING SEEDS

During the winter when it is cold, seeds and bulbs don't grow. They wait underground until the weather warms up in the spring.

HIDE AND SEEK

Cold, frosty weather can damage or kill small plants and flowers. Can you spot a flower with brown, frost-damaged edges?

HEY, WHAT AM I?

What can you see in this picture? Answer on page 29.

PLANT MAZE

Prove that plants grow towards light with this cool maze experiment.
You'll need:

Scissors and some sellotape

Shoebox and some extra card

A potted bean plant

STEP ONE

Cut two pieces of card the same height as the shoebox, but only half as wide as the narrow end of the box. Sellotape the pieces of card inside the box, one on the right and one on the left, dividing the box into thirds.

Ask an adult to help with any cutting.

STEP €O

Cut a large hole in one end of the shoebox.

STEP THREE

Stand the box on its end, and place the well-watered bean plant in the bottom.

STEP FOUR

Place the lid on the front of the box and tape it up around the edges, so that light can only get in through the hole in the top. After 5 days, take the lid off the front of the box.

How has the plant grown?

ANSWERS

Page 7 (cactus photo) — What am I? I'm a cactus plant

Page 7 (Plants spread) — Hide and Seek There are 4 daisies hiding

Page 9 — What am I? I'm the root hairs on a new plant shoot

Page 12 (Leaves spread) — Hide and Seek Holly leaves

Page 13 — What am I? I'm a lettuce

Page 15 — What am I? I'm the anther

Page 19

Hide and Seek Dandelion seed

Page 19

What am I?
I'm a plant bulb with a new bulblet growing and splitting off

Page 23

Hide and Seek A red maple leaf

Page 23

What am I?
I'm a pile of fallen leaves

Page 25

Hide and Seek Frost-damaged flower

Page 25

What am I?
I'm bananas on a banana tree

GLOSSARY

anther the part of the flower that holds the pollen

bulb a rounded, fleshy part that some types of plant sprout from

bulblet a new bulb that starts to grow from the side of another bulb

carbon dioxide one of the invisible gases that make up the air, also written as CO_2

deciduous tree a tree that loses all its leaves in winter

evergreen tree a tree that keeps its leaves in winter

fertiliser stuff that is added to soil to give nutrients to plants

flower the part of the plant where new seeds are made

flowering plant a plant that grows flowers

leaf the part of the plant that captures sunlight

mature fully grown

non-flowering plant a plant that does not grow flowers

nutrients substances needed for healthy growth

ovary the part of the flower where new seeds develop

oxygen a gas that is in the air

petal the colourful parts of the flower that attract insects

photosynthesis a process that plants use to make food from sunlight, water and the air

pollen the dust that flowers swap in order to make new seeds

root the part of the plant that grows underground

seed the part of the plant that grows into a new plant

seedling a seed that has sprouted but has not fully grown

species a specific type of plant or animal

stem the part of the plant that holds up the leaves and flowers

stigma a sticky pad that receives pollen from other plants

style a tube that holds up the stigma

trunk the woody stem of a tree

INDEX

Boom Science Series contents lists

ELECTRICITY

- ★ ELECTRICITY AND ENERGY
- ★ USING ELECTRICITY
- ★ YOUR TURN: Electricity hunt
- ★ NATURAL ELECTRICITY
- ★ BATTERIES
- ★ CIRCUITS
- ★ YOUR TURN: Make a battery
- ★ SWITCHES
- ★ MAKING ELECTRICITY
- ★ STAYING SAFE
- ★ YOUR TURN: Make a switch

FORCES

- ★ PUSHES AND PULLS
- ★ GRAVITY
- ★ WEIGHT
- ★ YOUR TURN: Forces at the playground
- ★ FRICTION
- ★ WATER RESISTANCE
- ★ AIR RESISTANCE
- ★ YOUR TURN: Make a parachute
- ★ MAGNETS
- ★ SIMPLE MACHINES
- ★ YOUR TURN: Make simple machines

HUMAN BODY
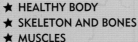

- ★ HEALTHY BODY
- ★ SKELETON AND BONES
- ★ MUSCLES
- ★ YOUR TURN: Make a model arm
- ★ DIGESTIVE SYSTEM
- ★ HEART AND BLOOD
- ★ BREATHING
- ★ YOUR TURN: How big are your lungs?
- ★ BRAIN AND NERVES
- ★ SENSES
- ★ YOUR TURN: Test your senses

LIGHT

- ★ LIGHT
- ★ NATURAL AND MAN-MADE LIGHT
- ★ LIGHT AND MATERIALS
- ★ YOUR TURN: Paint pictures with light
- ★ SHADOWS
- ★ SEEING
- ★ MIRRORS
- ★ YOUR TURN: Make shadow puppets
- ★ COLOUR
- ★ LIVING THINGS
- ★ YOUR TURN: Make a colour spinner

MATERIALS

- ★ MATERIALS
- ★ USING MATERIALS
- ★ PROPERTIES
- ★ YOUR TURN: Waterproof materials
- ★ NATURAL MATERIALS
- ★ MAN-MADE MATERIALS
- ★ YOUR TURN: Sorting materials
- ★ SOLIDS
- ★ LIQUIDS AND GASES
- ★ HEATING AND COOLING MATERIALS
- ★ YOUR TURN: Freezing materials

PLANTS

- ★ PLANTS
- ★ ROOTS AND STEMS
- ★ YOUR TURN: Colour change celery
- ★ LEAVES
- ★ FLOWERS
- ★ FRUIT
- ★ SEEDS AND BULBS
- ★ YOUR TURN: Grow a bulb in water
- ★ SUNLIGHT
- ★ WATER AND WARMTH
- ★ YOUR TURN: Plant maze

SEASONS

- ★ FOUR SEASONS
- ★ SPRING
- ★ SUMMER
- ★ YOUR TURN: Make a rain gauge
- ★ AUTUMN
- ★ WINTER
- ★ YOUR TURN: Make frost
- ★ ANIMALS
- ★ PLANTS
- ★ CELEBRATIONS
- ★ YOUR TURN: Build a bug hotel

SOUND

- ★ SOUND WAVES
- ★ HEARING
- ★ YOUR TURN: Improve your ears
- ★ MAKING SOUNDS
- ★ LOUD AND SOFT
- ★ HIGH AND LOW
- ★ YOUR TURN: Guess the sound
- ★ ECHOES
- ★ MUSIC
- ★ ANIMAL SOUNDS
- ★ YOUR TURN: Make music